CUBA
FACTS AND FIGURES

EXPLORING CUBA

CUBA
FACTS AND FIGURES

John Ziff

MC **MASON CREST**
PHILADELPHIA

Mason Crest
450 Parkway Drive, Suite D
Broomall, PA 19008
www.masoncrest.com

Printed and bound in the United States of America.

CPSIA Compliance Information: Batch #EC2017.
For further information, contact Mason Crest at 1-866-MCP-Book.

First printing
1 3 5 7 9 8 6 4 2

Library of Congress Cataloging-in-Publication Data

on file at the Library of Congress
ISBN: 978-1-4222-3810-3 (hc)
ISBN: 978-1-4222-7977-9 (ebook)

EXPLORING CUBA series ISBN: 978-1-4222-3808-0

QR CODES AND LINKS TO THIRD-PARTY CONTENT

TABLE OF CONTENTS

KEY ICONS TO LOOK FOR:

Words to understand: These words with their easy-to-understand definitions will increase the reader's understanding of the text while building vocabulary skills.

Sidebars: This boxed material within the main text allows readers to build knowledge, gain insights, explore possibilities, and broaden their perspectives by weaving together additional information to provide realistic and holistic perspectives.

Educational Videos: Readers can view videos by scanning our QR codes, providing them with additional educational content to supplement the text. Examples include news coverage, moments in history, speeches, iconic sports moments and much more!

Text-dependent questions: These questions send the reader back to the text for more careful attention to the evidence presented there.

Research projects: Readers are pointed toward areas of further inquiry connected to each chapter. Suggestions are provided for projects that encourage deeper research and analysis.

Series glossary of key terms: This back-of-the book glossary contains terminology used throughout this series. Words found here increase the reader's ability to read and comprehend higher-level books and articles in this field.

View of the Escambray Mountains near Trinidad. This range runs for about 50 miles (80 km) across central Cuba.

WORDS TO UNDERSTAND IN THIS CHAPTER

cay—a small, low island or reef consisting of sand or coral.

cordillera—a system of mountain ranges typically made up of a number of roughly parallel chains.

deciduous—referring to trees or shrubs that lose their leaves seasonally.

tributary—a stream or river that flows into a larger river.

THE LAND

With its white sand beaches and crystalline waters, its pristine rain forests and splendid colonial architecture, Cuba has been called "the Pearl of the Caribbean." It is the largest and northernmost of the Greater Antilles. That island group (which also includes Hispaniola, Jamaica, and Puerto Rico), along with the string of smaller islands that make up the Lesser Antilles, bounds the Caribbean Sea to the north and east.

Cuba's nearest international neighbor is Haiti. That country, which occupies the western half of the island of Hispaniola, lies slightly south and to the east of Cuba. At their closest point, Cuba and Haiti are separated by only about 60 miles (97 kilometers). To Cuba's south, at a distance of around 110 miles (177 km), is Jamaica. Mexico lies to Cuba's west.

The distance between the western tip of Cuba and the eastern tip of Mexico's Yucatán Peninsula is approximately 120 miles (193 km).

Situated to the north of Cuba is a country with which the island nation has had a tangled and troubled relationship: the United States. The Straits of Florida separates Cuba from southern Florida. About 90 miles (145 km) across the straits from northern Cuba lies Key West. It's at the end of the string of islands known as the Florida Keys, which since the early 1960s have been the destination for tens of thousands of Cubans trying to flee their country by sea. Miami, where a majority of Cubans who made it to U.S. soil ultimately settled, is roughly 230 miles (370 km) from Havana, Cuba's capital city.

AREA AND COASTLINE

The independent country of Cuba consists of one large island, which is also called Cuba, and several thousand surrounding islands and *cays*. With one exception, these surrounding islands are small. The exception is Isla de la Juventud, which covers 934 square miles (2,219 sq km). It's located south of the western part of the main island.

In all, Cuba has an area of approximately 42,803 square miles (110,860 sq km). That makes the country a little bit bigger than Tennessee.

The island of Cuba is long and relatively narrow. The island stretches in a generally northwest to southeast direction, from Cabo San Antonio in the west to Punta de Maisí in the east. The distance between those two points is approximately 750

Tourists enjoy the beach and clear water at Guardalavaca, a popular resort on Cuba's northern shore.

miles (1,207 km). The island's width varies from approximately 25 miles to 125 miles (40 to 201 km).

The island of Cuba has about 2,000 miles (3,218 km) of coastline. Isla de la Juventud and the country's other islands add about 330 additional miles (531 km) of coastline.

MAJOR TOPOGRAPHIC FEATURES

About two-thirds of Cuba's land surface consists of flat or rolling plains. These areas are mostly at low elevation. They average about 330 feet (100 meters) above sea level.

The Viñales Valley is located in western Cuba. It is dotted with large limestone outcrops that rise as high as 1,000 feet (300 meters).

Eastern Cuba is a mountainous region. The island's longest and highest mountain range, the Sierra Maestra, overlooks the southeastern coast. It dominates the province of Santiago de Cuba and extends into the neighboring province of Granma. The range, which is oriented in an east-west direction, runs about 150 miles (241 km) in total. The average elevation along the top of the range's long spine is around 4,920 feet (1,500 meters). At 6,476 feet (1,974 meters), Pico Turquino is both the tallest peak in the Sierra Maestra and the highest point in Cuba. The Sierra Maestra is heavily forested. It's also quite rugged, with steep slopes and plunging ravines.

Smaller mountain ranges, notably the Sierra de Nipe and the Sierra Cristal, cover the southern part of the province of Holguín and much of the province of Guantánamo. Holguín borders Santiago de Cuba to the north. Guantánamo, Cuba's easternmost province, borders Santiago de Cuba to the east. Pico Cristal, the highest mountain in the Sierra Cristal range, ranks as Cuba's second-highest peak. Its summit rises 4,039 feet (1,231 meters) above sea level.

Outside of the eastern part of the island, Cuba has two significant mountain ranges. The Sierra del Escambray, situated in south-central Cuba, covers about 2,500 square miles (6,475 sq km) in the provinces of Sancti Spíritus, Villa Clara, and Cienfuegos. The tallest peak in the range, at about 3,740 feet (1,140 m), is Pico San Juan.

The Cordillera de Guaniguanico is a string of low mountains and hills in western Cuba. It runs parallel to the island's northern coast for about 100 miles (160 km). The *cordillera* lies almost entirely within Cuba's westernmost province, Pinar del Río. A small section is in Artemisa, the province that borders Pinar del Río to the east. The Cordillera de Guaniguanico may not soar—its highest mountain, Pan de Guajaibón, reaches an elevation of just 2,293 feet (699 m). Nonetheless, the range offers vistas of dramatic beauty, including valleys dotted by steep, isolated, domelike limestone formations.

LAKES, RIVERS, AND WETLANDS

Inland, Cuba has relatively little open water. The largest natural lake, Laguna de Leche, has a surface area of only about 26 square miles (67 sq km). It's located in central Cuba's Ciego de Ávila Province. The man-made Zaza Reservoir, at approximately 44 square miles (114 sq km), is the largest freshwater body of water in Cuba. It's in Sancti Spíritus Province.

Cuba's rivers, of which there are approximately 200, are mostly short. The longest, at about 230 miles (370 km), is the Río Cauto. An important source of water for irrigation, it rises in the mountains of southeastern Cuba and winds through the provinces of Santiago de Cuba and Granma. Before emptying into the Gulf of Guacanayabo, the Cauto spreads out into a broad swath of wetlands.

Flowing 81 miles (130 km) across the eastern province of Guantánamo, the Toa is Cuba's second-longest river. It has dozens of *tributaries*. Other significant rivers include the

EDUCATIONAL VIDEO

Scan to see El Nicho Park, in the Sierra del Escambray, Cienfuegos Province:

El Nicho waterfall is part of the Topes de Collantes Natural Park, located in the Escambray Mountains in Cienfuegos Province.

Guamá, which is also in Guantánamo Province and which at 51 miles (82 km) is Cuba's third-longest river. The scenic Yumurí flows about 34 miles (54 km) before emptying into the Bay of Matanzas, along the northern coast of Cuba at the provincial capital of Matanzas. The Almendares, 29 miles (47 km) in length, cuts through Havana and is a source of drinking water for residents of the country's capital city.

Wetlands cover a significant portion of Cuba. According to recent estimates, around 8 percent to 9 percent of Cuba's total area consists of swamps, marshes, bogs, and the like. Scientists recognize the critically important ecological roles that healthy wetlands play—from providing habitat for diverse plant and

The Zapata Swamp is home to thousands of species of plants, birds, reptiles, and other animals. Some of these species can only be found in Cuba.

animal species, to filtering pesticides and other harmful chemicals out of water, to limiting floods and coastal erosion.

Cuba boasts the largest intact wetland in the Caribbean region. Called the Ciénaga de Zapata, or Zapata Swamp, it covers more than 1,600 square miles (4,144 sq km) of southern Matanzas Province. A national park protects the Zapata Swamp from development. It's part of an even bigger biosphere reserve established under a program run by UNESCO (the United Nations Educational, Scientific and Cultural Organization).

CLIMATE

Cuba's climate is classified as subtropical. Summers are hot and winters warm. Humidity, especially during the summer months, is very high. Areas along the northern coast are made more comfortable by the trade winds—prevailing winds that blow almost constantly from the northeast toward the equator. The southern part of the island tends to be a bit hotter than the northern part, with the highest temperatures typically recorded in Guantánamo Province. At higher elevations in the mountains, though, temperatures are considerably cooler.

Cuba doesn't experience four distinct seasons. Instead, the year is marked by a wet season and a dry season. The former, which lasts from May through October, sees about two-thirds of Cuba's annual rainfall. But rain is by no means constant during the wet season. It's not even a daily occurrence. In Havana, for instance, rainfall can be expected, on average, every third or fourth day during the wet season. There are some regional differences, but overall October is the wettest month in Cuba. On

THE GEOGRAPHY OF CUBA

Location: northwest Caribbean Sea, south of Florida

Area:
   Total: 42,803 sq miles (110,860 sq km)
   Land: 42,402 sq miles (109,820 sq km)
   Water: 401 sq miles (1,040 sq km)

Land boundaries: none (the United States leases a naval base at Guantánamo Bay)

Coastline: 2,330 miles (3,749 km)

Highest point: Pico Turquino, 6,476 feet (1,974 m)

Lowest point: Caribbean coast (sea level)

Sources: CIA World Factbook, 2017;
Merriam-Webster's Geographical Dictionary, 3rd ed. (2001).

average about 6.6 inches (16.8 centimeters) of rainfall can be expected during that month. Of the wet months, July typically receives the least rainfall, at slightly under 4 inches (10 cm). From mid-June through November, the island is susceptible to being hit by hurricanes.

June through October are the hottest months in Cuba. Nationwide, daily high temperatures during that time average about 86 to 88 degrees Fahrenheit (30 to 31 degrees Celsius). Daily lows average about 71°F to 75°F (22°C to 24°C).

Monthly rainfall from December to March averages only about 1.5 inches (3.8 cm). Average rainfall during the other two months of the dry season is substantially higher—about 2.2 inches (5.6 cm) in May, and 2.5 inches (6.3 cm) in November.

December, January, and February are the mildest months of the year in Cuba. Nationally, daytime highs average about 79°F to 81°F (26°C to 27°C). Nighttime low temperatures average about 64°F to 66°F (18°C to 19°C).

FLORA AND FAUNA

Cuba has a stunning variety of plant and animal species. Many species found in Cuba are found nowhere else in the world.

Biologists conservatively estimate that Cuba has more than 6,000 plant species. About half are believed to exist only in Cuba. These include, among many others, several types of palm trees, a species of pine, a cactus, and a variety of orchids and other flowering plants.

About one-quarter of Cuba's land is forested. Mangrove forests, the largest of which are in the Zapata Swamp, grow in coastal wetlands. *Deciduous* forests once covered much of the island's lowland and plains areas, but they have mostly been cleared for agriculture. Scattered areas of semi-deciduous forests—which are composed of a mix of broadleaf deciduous and evergreen trees—can be found in remote, hilly parts of Cuba. Pine forests cover some mountain slopes. Rain forests flourish in areas of eastern Cuba.

Cuba is home to more than 200 species of reptiles and amphibians. They range from the endangered Cuban crocodile, a fearsome predator that can top 12 feet (3.6 meters) in length and reach 300 pounds, to the world's tiniest known frog,

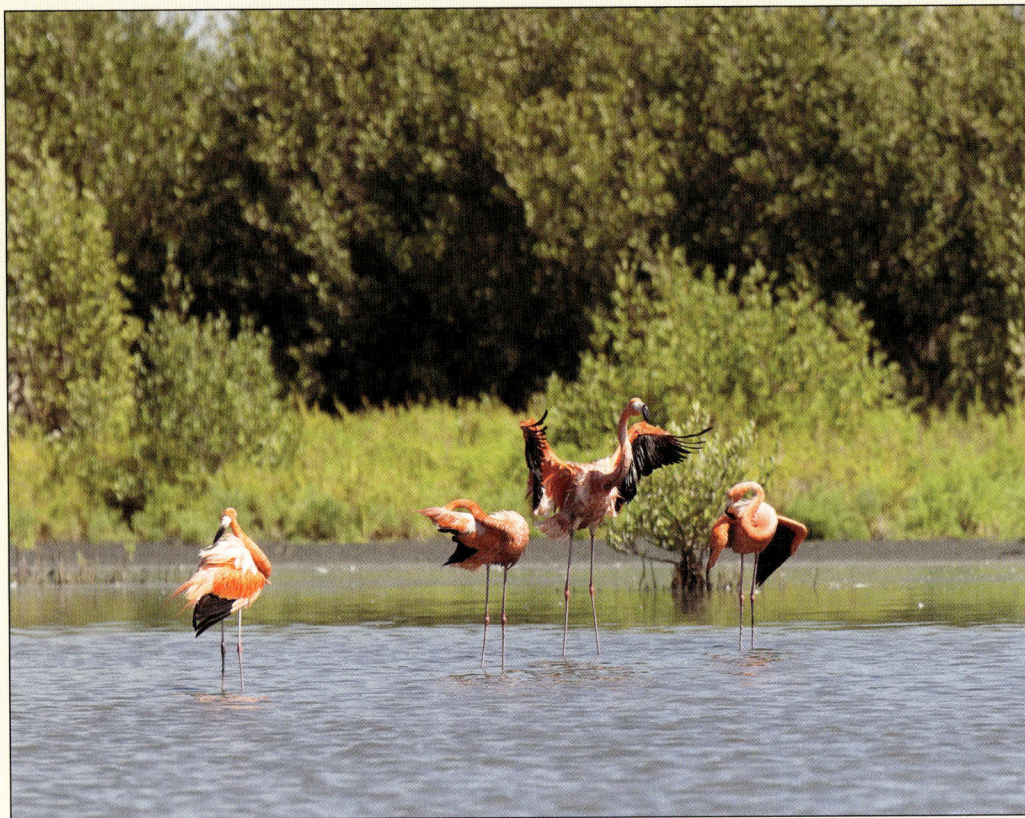

A group of Caribbean flamingos stand in a lake in Cuba.

which at 0.4 inches (1 cm) long could easily fit on the surface of an American dime.

Of the nearly 370 bird species that can be seen in Cuba, about two dozen are found nowhere else. These include the world's smallest bird, the bee hummingbird, which is about as big as a U.S. quarter; the gorgeously colored Cuban tody; and the Cuban trogon, the country's national bird.

No large land mammals are native to Cuba. However, manatees and dugongs live in some of the island's rivers and coastal swamps. Cuba is home to many species of bats. It also has a wide variety of rodents. One of the island's more interesting mammals is the endangered Cuban solenodon (also known as the almiquí), which looks a bit like a shrew. Its saliva is venomous, which is highly unusual for mammals.

Scientists recognize Cuba as among the most biologically diverse islands in the world. Fortunately, much of Cuba's land has been set aside for conservation. In fact, national parks, regional parks, and other nature reserves account for about one-fifth of Cuba's total land area.

TEXT-DEPENDENT QUESTIONS

1. Which country is Cuba's nearest neighbor?
2. Name the longest and highest mountain range in Cuba.
3. Which Cuban province typically records the highest temperatures?

RESEARCH PROJECT

Use the Internet to read about wildlife in Cuba. Choose an animal that interests you. Then do some additional research and write a one-page report.

Longtime Cuban leader Fidel Castro (1926–2016) speaks at the United Nations. Castro led a revolution that seized power in 1959, and he subsequently implemented a communist regime that still rules Cuba today.

📖 WORDS TO UNDERSTAND IN THIS CHAPTER

annex—to take possession of territory and incorporate it into an established country or state.

conquistador—a leader in the Spanish conquests of the New World.

coup—a sudden seizure of power through force or the threat of force.

embargo—an order by a government banning commerce with another state.

indigenous—native to a place; relating to the original inhabitants of an area or region.

nationalize—to transfer an industry from private to state ownership or control.

A BRIEF HISTORY OF CUBA

Based on evidence from recent excavations, archaeologists believe that humans have lived on the island of Cuba since at least 2700 BCE—and perhaps much longer. When Europeans first arrived in the Western Hemisphere, Cuba was home to an estimated 100,000 native people. They came from three main *indigenous* groups, the largest of which were the Taíno. Numbering an estimated 60,000, the Taíno occupied the eastern two-thirds of the island by the late 1400s. They fished, hunted, grew crops, and lived in villages ruled by leaders called caciques.

Christopher Columbus claimed Cuba for the king and queen of Spain in October 1492, during his first voyage to the New World. However, two decades would pass before the Spanish made a concerted effort to explore the island and subdue its inhabitants. That effort was led by a *conquistador* named Diego Velázquez de Cuéllar.

In 1511, Velázquez and an army of more than 300 Spanish soldiers set sail from the neighboring island of Hispaniola, which at the time was the site of Spain's largest New World colony. The expedition landed in eastern Cuba. There, Velázquez established the first Spanish settlement on the island, Baracoa.

Velázquez apparently wasn't expecting much resistance from Cuba's indigenous population, as previous Spanish contacts with the island's native inhabitants had been friendly.

Christopher Columbus discovered Cuba during his first voyage to the New World, landing on the island on October 28, 1492. He claimed the land for the king and queen of Spain, who had financed his voyage.

Taíno artifacts on display in a museum. The Taíno were Native Americans who lived on Cuba and other islands in the Caribbean before the arrival of the Spanish. However, their culture was mostly destroyed by the Spanish conquistadores during the first three decades of the fifteenth century.

Some Taíno villages did in fact welcome the conquistador and his men. But a Taíno cacique named Hatuey mounted a fierce struggle to repel the Spanish invaders.

Both sides fought ferociously. But the Spanish often descended into barbarity, as Bartolomé de Las Casas—a priest who accompanied the Velázquez expedition—would later chronicle. One gruesome incident Las Casas witnessed occurred at a Taíno village that by the priest's reckoning contained about 2,500 souls. Around 100 Spanish soldiers entered the village one evening. The Taíno brought them food, but the soldiers suddenly drew their swords and, Las Casas wrote, "began to rip open the bellies and, to cut and kill those lambs—

men, women, children, and old folk . . . so that a stream of blood was running" and all of the villagers lay slaughtered.

By 1514, the Spanish had completed the conquest of Cuba and established a handful of settlements on the island. They forced indigenous people to work on plantations and in mines.

STRATEGIC IMPORTANCE

Diego Velázquez, appointed Cuba's first royal governor by the Spanish crown, envisioned Cuba as the center of Spain's New World empire. He tried to entice large numbers of Spaniards to immigrate to the colony. His efforts met with some success— but that success would prove temporary.

By 1521, Hernán Cortés—a former aide–turned–rival of Velázquez—had conquered the mighty Aztecs of Mexico, thereby expanding the Spanish Empire into the mainland of North America. Mexico contained vast amounts of silver and gold, and the prospect of getting rich there—or, a bit later, in South America—drew Spanish colonists away from Cuba.

By 1550, Cuba was a backwater of Spain's New World empire. The island's capital, Santiago de Cuba, was home to only about 150 Spanish colonists. A handful of other small settlements on the island brought the total number of Spanish colonists in Cuba to roughly 700.

A similar number of enslaved Africans lived on the island. They replaced the indigenous people as a source of forced labor. Cuba's native population had been decimated by mistreatment at the hands of the Spanish and by disease. Like the other indigenous peoples of the New World, they had no natu-

The Spanish used slave labor to build large fortresses, such as Castillo de los Tres Reyes Magos del Morro at the entrance to Havana's harbor. The fort, known as El Morro, was constructed in the late sixteenth century to defend Havana from attacks by pirates and Spain's enemies.

ral immunity to deadly diseases brought by the Europeans, such as smallpox, measles, and influenza.

By the late 1500s, Spanish authorities had come to recognize Cuba's strategic importance. The island stood astride the main shipping lanes into the Caribbean Sea and the Gulf of Mexico—and hence the approaches to Spain's mainland colonies. Those colonies were generating untold riches, including gold, silver, and gems. But that treasure had to be transported across the Atlantic Ocean to the mother country. And

Spain's European rivals—France, England, the Netherlands—were intent on disrupting the flow. Isolated, unprotected cargo ships were preyed on by foreign naval vessels, privateers, and pirates. Even more alarming, from the Spanish point of view, were foreign raids of Cuba, some of which resulted in the plundering and burning of Spanish settlements. If Spanish colonists could be driven from Cuba, a rival country might then occupy the island. From this position, the rival country could effectively choke off Spanish shipping through the Caribbean.

Spanish authorities devised measures to counter these threats. To defend Cuba, they garrisoned soldiers on the island. To protect shipping, they instituted a convoy system. Each spring a huge fleet of cargo ships—accompanied by Spanish warships—would depart Spain with supplies for the New World colonies. Each summer the ships, loaded with treasure from the colonies, would assemble in Havana's harbor for the return voyage to Spain.

As a result of these policies, the number of people in Cuba—both Spanish and enslaved Africans—grew. By the first decade of the 17th century, the island's population reached about 20,000. By the turn of the next century, it stood at approximately 50,000. Havana, which had grown quite prosperous because of its role as an imperial hub, was home to about half of Cuba's people.

PLANTATIONS AND SLAVERY

In 1762, near the end of a wide-reaching conflict known as the Seven Years' War, British forces captured Havana and effectively took control of Cuba. The British presence would be brief—

a peace treaty returned Cuba to Spain in 1763—but it would prove significant. The British brought some 10,000 African slaves to Cuba. The intent was for them to toil on big sugarcane plantations that British colonists would establish.

At this point agriculture in Cuba was fairly limited in scale. But during the final decades of the 1700s and the first decades of the 1800s, a series of international developments made the sort of plantation economy envisioned by the British a reality

This watercolor image created in 1595 shows African slaves processing sugarcane on a Spanish plantation in the Caribbean.

in Cuba. Among those developments was the Haitian Revolution, which convulsed the French colony of Saint-Domingue for more than a decade, beginning in 1791. The revolution devastated agricultural exports—and Saint-Domingue had been responsible for up to 40 percent of the sugar consumed in Europe, and more than half the coffee.

Cuba, where many French planters fled to escape the Haitian Revolution, was able to take advantage of the opening in the export market. Vast plantations, particularly ones on which sugarcane was cultivated, were established on the island.

During the 1800s, Cuba became the world's leading producer of sugar. Planters on the island became very wealthy. Spain, too, reaped a financial windfall from taxes.

But Cuba's plantation economy required a huge supply of labor. Most of it was provided by enslaved Africans. Between 1800 and 1867—when the slave trade to Cuba ended—more than a million Africans, mostly from West Africa, were brought to the island in chains. Slavery in Cuba would be completely abolished only with an 1886 decree by the Spanish crown.

LONG ROAD TO INDEPENDENCE

By the first years of the 19th century, Spain's colonies were simmering with discontent. Many colonists—especially prosperous whites of Spanish descent who'd been born in the Western Hemisphere—chafed at being ruled by a distant mother country. They resented the fact that their political rights were limited, and that the top positions in colonial administra-

Sugar became one of Cuba's most important export products in the nineteenth century. Slaves were needed to harvest and process sugarcane.

tions were reserved for persons born in Spain. They believed it unfair that Spain placed its economic interests before theirs.

Events in Europe would help cause resentments in Spanish America to boil over into revolution. In 1808 Napoleon Bonaparte, the French emperor, invaded Spain and forced King Ferdinand VII to give up the throne. Napoleon installed his brother, Joseph Bonaparte, as king of Spain.

Many colonists in Spanish America refused to accept Spain's new king as legitimate, however. And this magnified their other grievances, spurring colonists into action. Wars of independence soon broke out across Spanish America. Within two decades, Spain had lost almost the entirety of its once-vast empire in the Western Hemisphere. Puerto Rico and Cuba were all that remained.

In Cuba, a significant amount of support developed for the idea of breaking away from Spain. But Spanish authorities were determined to hold on to the island at all costs.

In 1850, a military expedition aimed at ousting the Spanish from Cuba was mounted by a general named Narciso López. López, who originally hailed from Venezuela, had settled in Cuba before being forced to flee to the United States because of his anti-Spain activities. A supporter of slavery, López hoped to convince the United States to *annex* Cuba, and to admit the island into the Union as a slave state. Influential Southerners were receptive to this idea, and they provided financial backing with which López raised and outfitted a 600-man army. A few of these men were Cuban exiles. Most were American soldiers-for-hire from the South. López's army sailed from New Orleans in May 1850. Shortly after landing in Cuba, however, the invaders withdrew in the face of determined Spanish opposition.

López mounted a similar expedition the following year. But this time Spanish troops captured and executed the general, along with the bulk of his force.

Some slaveholding Cuban planters still hoped the United States would annex the island. And, in fact, that was a goal of James Buchanan, U.S. president from 1857 to 1861. But, with the country bitterly divided over the issue of slavery, Buchanan couldn't push annexation of Cuba through Congress. The Civil War (1861–1865) ended slavery in the United States, effectively eliminating any possibility of a U.S. annexation of slaveholding Cuba.

Still, some Cubans continued to hold out hope that the United States might annex the island. One such person was a wealthy lawyer and sugar planter named Carlos Manuel de Céspedes. In October 1868, Céspedes freed his slaves, proclaimed Cuba independent, and initiated a rebellion against Spanish rule. Within a year, as many as 30,000 Cubans had taken up arms in support of this cause. But while the rebels succeeded in capturing most of eastern Cuba, a decade of fighting produced a stalemate—and the United States declined to annex the island or otherwise intervene in the struggle. The Ten Years' War, as the conflict came to be called, ended with the signing of the Pact of Zanjón. Under this treaty, Spain committed to certain reforms, including the phasing out of slavery in Cuba.

Carlos Manuel de Céspedes (1819–1874) was a Cuban planter who declared Cuban independence from Spain in 1868. He is sometimes called the "Father of Cuba."

But for many Cubans, the dream of independence hadn't died. Another rebellion, which would come to be called the

Little War, broke out in August 1879. Spanish troops had quashed this rebellion by September 1880.

In 1892, Cuban exiles living in New York and Philadelphia founded the Cuban Revolutionary Party. Its leading figure was the writer and philosopher José Martí. Martí visited Cuban communities in the United States, the Caribbean, and Central

This statue of José Martí stands in the main square of Cienfuegos. Martí (1853–1895) was an important leader in the fight for Cuban independence from Spain during the late nineteenth century. Although he was killed at the Battle of Dos Ríos in May 1895, the rebels he had inspired continued resisting the Spanish.

America, drumming up support for another fight for Cuban independence.

In March and April 1895, two veteran generals, Antonio Maceo and Máximo Gómez, landed in eastern Cuba to liberate the island. Martí, serving as an aide to Gómez, was killed in action in May.

The Spanish fielded vastly more troops, but the rebels' guerrilla tactics proved effective. By early 1896, the Spanish had begun forcing Cuban civilians into "reconcentration" camps. This was to prevent civilians from helping the rebels, but conditions in the camps were appalling, and many people died from disease or starvation.

Despite their harsh treatment of civilians, and despite their numerical superiority, Spanish forces were unable to stamp out the uprising. While they controlled Cuba's major cities and towns, the rebels held the countryside. By late 1897, Spain had crafted a plan by which Cuba would be granted self-rule in domestic matters while still remaining part of the Spanish Empire. The plan took effect on January 1, 1898. But many Cubans continued to insist on full independence, and within weeks rioting erupted in Havana.

The United States had extensive commercial interests in Cuba. Most of the island's sugar mills, for example, were American owned. To protect U.S. property, President William McKinley dispatched the battleship *Maine* to Havana. On February 15, 1898, the *Maine* exploded while at anchor in the city's harbor.

A U.S. naval court of inquiry blamed the explosion, and the resulting deaths of 260 American sailors, on a Spanish mine.

Though most historians today are skeptical of that conclusion, it led the U.S. Congress to pass a war declaration against Spain on April 25.

The Spanish-American War proved brief. On August 12, 1898, Spain and the United States signed an armistice. Having been defeated decisively, Spain agreed to give up Cuba, as well as Puerto Rico and two colonies in the Pacific, Guam and the Philippines.

STUNTED REPUBLIC

For several years after the Spanish-American War, the United States administered Cuba under a military occupation. In May 1902, the island officially gained independence as the Republic of Cuba. But there was a catch: Cuba had to accept an American law known as the Platt Amendment, which gave the United States the legal right to intervene in Cuban affairs under certain circumstances (for example, if political instability threatened life or property). And, in fact, American soldiers were dispatched to Cuba on four separate occasions before the Platt Amendment was finally repealed in 1934.

The previous year, Cuba's unpopular and increasingly despotic president, Gerardo Machado, had been forced from office—in part through the efforts of Sumner Welles, the U.S. ambassador to Cuba. Amid the instability, an army sergeant named Fulgencio Batista spearheaded a military *coup*, dubbed the "Revolt of the Sergeants" because it involved noncommissioned officers like himself.

Batista promoted himself to chief of staff of the Cuban army. From that position he exercised power behind the scenes, installing and removing a series of puppet presidents throughout the remainder of the 1930s.

In 1940, after Cuba had adopted a new constitution, Batista ran for president himself. And, in a generally free and fair election, he won convincingly. Batista stepped aside when his four-year term was over—the Cuban Constitution of 1940 prohibited presidents from serving consecutive terms—even though voters dealt his preferred successor a

Cuban dictator Fulgencio Batista, pictured here waving to crowds during a parade, dominated Cuban politics from the 1930s until early 1959.

defeat at the ballot box. Free elections, and another peaceful transfer of power, took place again in 1948. Cuba, it seemed, was on the path to a stable democracy.

But Fulgencio Batista decided to run for president again in 1952. And when an opinion poll showed him trailing badly, he seized power in a coup and cancelled the elections.

During this stint in power, Batista's corruption was blatant and breathtaking. While millions of Cuban peasants lived in extreme poverty, he looted the government's coffers, amassing a personal fortune estimated at $300 million. As opposition to his dictatorship grew, he became increasingly ruthless. His security forces arrested opponents and suspected opponents, torturing and killing thousands.

Revolutionary leader Fidel Castro speaks to the media shortly after gaining power in Cuba, 1959.

An early, and inept, attempt to overthrow Batista occurred in Santiago de Cuba in July 1953. The leader of that plot, a lawyer named Fidel Castro, served a short prison term before going into exile in Mexico to plan another rebellion.

In December 1956, Castro returned to Cuba and, with a small group of revolutionaries, began waging a guerrilla campaign from camps in the rugged Sierra Maestra. Batista's forces collapsed in late 1958, and the dictator fled the country on January 1, 1959.

COMMUNIST CUBA

While the revolution was under way, Castro had promised to bring democracy to Cuba. He'd expressed his dedication to the Constitution of 1940, which guaranteed a broad range of rights and freedoms, including freedom of expression and belief.

Castro made no attempt to establish a democracy once in power. Instead, he created a communist dictatorship—which he personally led for five decades. When he finally stepped down in 2008, power passed to his brother Raúl.

The Castro regime muzzled dissent every bit as thoroughly as had Batista. Critics of the government were harassed and imprisoned. Independent media were shut down, as the government sought to control all information to which Cuban citizens had access.

Communism, the ideology that guided the Castro government, anticipates a future of complete economic equality. In that future, according to communist theory, resources will be shared equally by all members of society. Ultimately the state itself will become unnecessary and will disappear. Before that final stage of history, communist theory holds, society must first go through socialism. During this stage of historical development, some inequality continues to exist. But the state controls the production and distribution of goods, and does so—in theory, at least—for the benefit of everyone.

In keeping with communist principles, the Castro regime brought the entire Cuban economy under state control. This occurred in stages, with the government *nationalizing* foreign-owned businesses first, then taking large Cuban landholdings and businesses, then medium-sized landholdings and businesses. The government completed its takeover of the economy with a 1968 law that

EDUCATIONAL VIDEO

Scan here for a short summary of U.S.-Cuba relations since 1959:

This reconnaissance photo taken in November 1962 by an American spy plane shows Soviet nuclear missiles and launchers being unloaded at the port of Mariel. After a tense two-week showdown, known as the Cuban Missile Crisis, the Soviet Union agreed to remove its missiles from Cuba in exchange for secret U.S. concessions.

made private ownership of even small businesses (such as barbershops and food stands) illegal. In essence, all Cuban workers had become employees of the state.

Historians disagree about whether Fidel Castro had always intended to make Cuba a communist state. It wasn't until May 1961 that Castro declared Cuba a "socialist country." And that declaration came just two weeks after the United States had attempted to overthrow his government by landing (at a place called the Bay of Pigs) a force of Cuban exiles armed and trained by the U.S. Central Intelligence Agency.

U.S. policy makers had become alarmed not only by the Castro government's seizure of American-owned businesses but also by its apparent lean toward the world's most powerful communist country, the Union of Soviet Socialist Republics. Cuba and the USSR—the main foe of the United States in the post–World War II struggle known as the Cold War—signed a trade agreement in February 1960. They established formal diplomatic relations a few months later. The United States severed its diplomatic relations with Cuba in January 1961 and

U.S. president Barack Obama shakes hands with Cuban leader Raúl Castro. In 2015, years of negotiation between the Obama administration and the Castro government resulted in the restoration of diplomatic relations between the United States and Cuba.

A U.S. Coast Guard cutter intercepts Cuban migrants in the Florida Strait. The migrants were drifting in a raft made of 55-gallon drums, hoping to reach Florida. They were returned to Cuba.

banned almost all U.S. trade with the island in February 1962. Diplomatic relations were finally reestablished in 2015, but the U.S. trade *embargo* remained in place at that time.

From its inception, the U.S. embargo was a significant blow to Cuban economic prospects. Over the decades, generous aid from the USSR blunted, but by no means negated, the embargo's effects. However, in 1991 the USSR collapsed, leaving Cuba without aid upon which it had come to rely, and plunging the island into an extended period of severe economic distress. Although that crisis was over by 2000, Cuba's economy has continued to struggle in the 21st century.

Whether to seek better economic opportunities or to escape government repression, more than 1.5 million Cubans have left their homeland since the revolution brought Fidel Castro to power in 1959. Most Cuban emigrants settled in the United States, and especially southern Florida.

The bulk of the exodus occurred in waves coinciding with periods when the Castro regime permitted citizens to leave the island (though not necessarily without first subjecting those citizens to onerous treatment). Until 2013, it was a crime to leave the island without a government-issued exit permit, and those permits were difficult to obtain and cost more than ordinary Cubans could afford. Still, over the years tens of thousands of Cubans risked prison sentences—and death at sea—by attempting to cross the Straits of Florida in small boats or homemade rafts.

TEXT-DEPENDENT QUESTIONS

1. Name the cacique who led Taíno resistance to the Spanish conquest of Cuba.
2. What incident led to the Spanish-American War? Where and when did that incident occur?
3. Which country provided Cuba with economic aid from the 1960s through the 1980s?

RESEARCH PROJECT

Using a library or the Internet, research the life of Cuban revolutionary leader and dictator Fidel Castro. Prepare a timeline of the major events.

The National Capitol building is a Havana landmark. It was the home of Cuba's legislature from 1929 until Fidel Castro took power in 1959. The building housed Cuban government agencies until 2010, when it was declared a national monument and closed for a major renovation.

WORDS TO UNDERSTAND IN THIS CHAPTER

chief of state—the formal head of a nation, as distinct from the head of government.

decree—an edict or order that usually carries the force of law.

judiciary—a system of courts of law; the judges serving on those courts.

rubber stamp—a person or organization that gives automatic approval to the decisions of others, without proper consideration.

GOVERNMENT

In the early 1980s, in the midst of the Cold War, there were about 20 communist states in the world. Only a handful remain today, and Cuba is among them.

Cuba's Communist Party, the Partido Comunista de Cuba (PCC), maintains a monopoly on governmental power. Indeed, in 1992—in the wake of communism's collapse in the Soviet Union and Eastern Europe—Cuba amended its constitution to enshrine the PCC's role as "the highest leading force of society and of the state, which organizes and guides the common effort toward the goals of the construction of socialism and the progress toward a communist society." That amendment remains in effect today.

The leader of the PCC—who carries the title first secretary of the Communist Party—has also been the actual leader of

Cuba, occupying the top post in the Cuban government. The first secretary heads the Politburo, a committee of the most powerful officials in the Communist Party. The Politburo, whose membership varies from around 15 to around 25, is arguably the most influential decision-making body in Cuba.

EXECUTIVE AUTHORITY

In Cuba, as in the United States, the functions of *chief of state* and head of government are filled by one individual. That individual serves as president of Cuba's Council of State and president of Cuba's Council of Ministers. The Council of State and Council of Ministers have a first vice-president, who serves as the number-two official.

When declining health forced him to relinquish power after nearly a half-century as Cuba's top leader, Fidel Castro hand-picked his brother Raúl to succeed him. Raúl Castro, a lieutenant of his brother's during the revolution, held the posts of minister of the armed forces and first vice-president of both the Council of Ministers and Council of State before ascending to the top spot.

Technically, the Cuban president serves a five-year term. But there are no limits on the number of consecutive terms a person may serve. And because the president is selected not by voters but by the Council of State—which the president heads—the same person may hold the presidency indefinitely, until age and infirmity take their inevitable toll. Fidel Castro certainly demonstrated that. However, Raúl Castro was already 76 years old when the Council of State unanimously elected him president in 2008. Shortly after his unanimous reelection in 2013, he announced that he would step down in February 2018, at the end of his second term.

Most observers expected that Raúl Castro would be succeeded by Miguel Díaz-Canel, who in 2013 was elevated to first vice-president of the Council of State and the Council of Ministers. Born in 1960, Díaz-Canel wasn't even alive during the Cuban Revolution. Whether he would generally continue the course set by the revolutionary generation—or whether he would wield nearly as much power as had the Castros—remained to be seen.

The Council of State, which selects Cuba's president, is itself chosen by Cuba's legislature. But, under the Castros at least, the legislature invariably bent to the will of the president. Thus

The buildings that house the Cuban Ministry of the Interior (left) and the Ministry of Communications (right) are located on Revolution Square in Havana. On the exterior of these government buildings are enormous steel sculptures of Ernesto "Che" Guevara and Camilo Cienfuegos, two heroes of the Cuban Revolution.

French president Francois Hollande (right) welcomes Raúl Castro at the Elysée Palace during the Cuban leader's state visit to France in 2016.

members of the Council of State have been reliable allies of the country's top leader. The Cuban Constitution specifies that the Council of State consist of 31 individuals. In addition to the president and first vice-president, there are five vice-presidents, a secretary, and 23 ordinary members. During times when Cuba's legislature isn't in session—and that's typically most of the year—the Council of State has legislative authority.

Cuba's Council of Ministers is somewhat akin to the Cabinet of the U.S. president. In addition to the president and first vice-president, it includes the heads of more than two dozen national ministries (for example, agriculture, the armed forces, culture, industry) and institutes (responsible, for example, for sports and for radio and television broadcasting). The Council of Ministers is charged with implementing policies and enforcing laws. It also submits economic plans to Cuba's legislature for approval.

THE LEGISLATURE

Cuba's legislature is called the National Assembly of People's Power (in Spanish, La Asamblea Nacional del Poder Popular). It's a unicameral, or single-chamber, body. National Assembly deputies serve five-year terms.

In theory, the National Assembly is a powerful institution. According to the Cuban Constitution, it's the supreme organ of the state and has sole law-making authority.

In practice, however, the power of the National Assembly is quite limited. Normally, it meets twice a year, with each of those sessions lasting only a few days. And, as noted earlier, legislative authority is held by the Council of State when the National Assembly isn't in session. Moreover, the president may issue *decrees* that carry the force of law—and both Castros made ample use of that power. Typically, the National Assembly spends much of its semiannual legislative sessions approving—unanimously—laws, decrees, and policies handed down from the Council of State or the president. This has led critics to suggest that Cuba's legislature amounts to little more than a *rubber stamp*.

The National Assembly has more than 600 seats. The precise number varies because of Cuba's unusual electoral system.

Cuban citizens cannot simply decide they want to run for the National Assembly, collect signatures, and get on the ballot. Rather, there are two mechanisms by which candidates considered suitable to serve are put forward. Each accounts for about half of the potential deputies in the National Assembly. First, public meetings are held under the auspices of municipalities. At these meetings, voters suggest candidates, who move forward in the process if a majority of the voters present at the meeting approve. Second, candidates are suggested by nominating assemblies, which are composed of representatives of "mass organizations" (such as the Federation of Cuban Women; the Federation of Cuban University Students; and the Committees for the Defense of the Revolution, neighborhood-level groups charged with monitoring everyone for possible antigovernment sentiment).

Once the municipalities and the nominating assemblies have developed lists of potential candidates, those candidates are vetted by the National Candidature Commission. The commission may reject anyone for any reason, including suspicion that the person might be insufficiently devoted to communist ideals, and its decisions are final.

The slate of candidates approved by the National Candidature Commission includes just one candidate for every seat in the National

EDUCATIONAL VIDEO

Scan here to view La Asamblea Nacional del Poder Popular in session:

A Cuban police officer patrols a street in Havana.

Assembly. Each voting district is allotted two to five seats. Voters may either approve a candidate by checking that person's name, or withhold their support by leaving the ballot blank. Any candidate whose name is checked on a majority of ballots wins the seat.

Cuban citizens age 16 and older are eligible to vote, though 18 is the minimum age for deputies in the National Assembly. Members of Cuba's provincial assemblies (Cuba has 15 provinces) are nominated and elected in a similar fashion. But Cubans as young as 16 may serve in a provincial legislature.

THE JUDICIARY

Cuba's judicial system is composed of three levels of courts, in addition to a separate system of military justice. Municipal courts make up the lowest level of the *judiciary*, followed by provincial courts. The People's Supreme Court is Cuba's highest court.

The Cuban Constitution supposedly ensures an independent judiciary. However, several factors make Cuban judges highly susceptible to political pressures. For one thing, judges serve for specified terms rather than receiving lifetime appointments, and they may be removed if their decisions run contrary to the desires of the president or Council of State. Unlike, for example, the Supreme Court of the United States, the People's Supreme Court has no authority to decide what is legal under the Cuban Constitution. That power rests with the National Assembly.

In addition, the Cuban Constitution expressly states that "none of the freedoms which are recognized for citizens may be exercised . . . contrary to the existence and objectives of the Socialist state, or contrary to the decision of the Cuban people to build socialism and communism." Further, a prison term is specified for any person who "incites against the social order."

Cuba's judiciary thus offers no protection for citizens who speak out against the government. The regime retains virtually unlimited discretion to define the acceptable limits of political dissent. And it has the tools to punish Cubans who challenge those limits.

TEXT-DEPENDENT QUESTIONS

1. What political party holds all governing authority in Cuba?
2. What is the Politburo?
3. What is the name of Cuba's legislature?

RESEARCH PROJECT

An English translation of the Cuban Constitution is available at:

http://www.constitutionnet.org/files/Cuba%20Constitution.pdf

Read the first chapter. Did you find anything similar to what is in the United States Constitution? Anything that is dramatically different? Write down your observations.

Ownership of this oil refinery in Cienfuegos is shared between the Cuban and Venezuelan governments. Cuba benefitted from a 2000 agreement with Venezuela enabling the island to purchase oil at favorable prices, which helped to support Cuba's economy.

WORDS TO UNDERSTAND IN THIS CHAPTER

collective farm—a farm, especially in a communist country, that is controlled by the government and worked by many farmers.

entrepreneur—a person who organizes, manages, and assumes the risks of a business.

gross domestic product (GDP)—the total value of goods and services produced in a country in a one-year period.

heavy industry—industry that requires large manufacturing facilities and machinery, such as steelmaking, shipbuilding, and automobile manufacturing.

subsidize—to support another government, group, or individual financially, especially by paying part of the cost of something.

THE ECONOMY

By the 1950s, on the cusp of the Cuban Revolution, Cuba was among the most prosperous countries in Latin America and the Caribbean. As was the case with other countries of the region, in Cuba land ownership was concentrated in the hands of a relatively small number of very wealthy families. However, Cuba also had a large and flourishing urban middle class, which enjoyed a standard of living comparable to that of middle classes in European countries such as Spain and France.

But extreme poverty existed in Cuba's countryside. Multitudes of landless peasants could find work—and difficult, low-paying work at that—only during the months when plantations needed a big supply of labor to harvest their sugarcane, tobacco, or coffee crops. For the rest of the year, peasant laborers and their families had to subsist on the meager wages obtained during the harvest.

Fidel Castro and his revolutionaries promised to make life better for Cuba's peasants. And they delivered. The Castro government took Cuba's big plantations from their private owners, gave land to peasants, and ultimately set up state-run *collective farms* on which former peasants would be guaranteed steady employment. Before the revolution, about half of Cuba's children didn't attend school. The Castro government made education—from grade school through university—free for all citizens, opening up opportunities that the children of the rural poor had never enjoyed. Free, universal health care also dramatically improved the lot of the country's poorest people.

If the Castro government dramatically reduced extreme poverty, its decades-long pursuit of communism also resulted in lost opportunities for broad-based economic development. There are various methods for assessing economic development, and by most measures Cuba today ranks among the world's middle-income countries. Nevertheless, Cubans' standard of living now lags far behind that of Latin America and the Caribbean as a whole.

ECONOMIC MISMANAGEMENT

In implementing socialism, Cuba experienced economic pitfalls common to other communist states. Among them was the inefficiency that invariably accompanied central planning, in which the state determines how to allocate resources, which goods are produced, and how those goods are distributed. Worker productivity was another chronic problem: with

A government ration store in Bayamo. The selection of merchandise available in these stores is often very limited. Cubans are used to going to different stores, and sometimes even different towns, in order to find even basic staples they need to survive.

employment guaranteed by the state and compensation not tied to performance, individual incentives to work hard tended to be weak. Over the long haul, communist states found capitalist countries (like the United States) outstripping them in innovation and economic growth.

But above and beyond the limitations of a socialist model of development, economic mismanagement was a hallmark of the Castro regime. Cuba, particularly in the first decade after the revolution, careened from one economic misadventure to another. In the early 1960s, Fidel Castro sought to make Cuba a powerhouse of *heavy industry*. That dream—which was never realistic because of the high cost of importing all the nec-

Farmers stand in a tobacco field in the Viñales valley. Ideal soil and growing conditions for tobacco help make Cuban cigars renowned across the world.

essary raw materials—had been abandoned by the middle of the decade. Castro decided Cuba needed to diversify the agricultural sector, which he believed was overly dependent on sugar production. Across the island, large swaths of sugarcane fields were uprooted and the land planted with other crops. Amid disappointing yields, however, Castro suddenly reversed himself. He decided that Cuba should focus almost exclusively on sugar. He announced that in 1970, Cuba would produce a record-setting 10 million tons of sugar, declaring it a "moral commitment" of the Cuban people not to "fall short by even a single gram." But despite a massive, disruptive mobilization of Cuban society, sugar production fell way short of Castro's goal.

THE "SPECIAL PERIOD"

The sugar debacle did considerable damage to Cuba's overall economy. Fortunately for the Castro regime, and for the Cuban people, in 1972 the USSR dramatically increased its economic aid to Cuba. The aid kept Cuba's economy afloat.

In the late 1980s, however, the USSR scaled back economic assistance to Cuba. And, when the USSR broke apart in 1991, all aid to the island ceased. Cuba's economy spiraled downward. *Gross domestic product* (GDP) plunged more than 35 percent in just a few years.

Deprivation was nothing new for Cubans under the Castro regime. But at no time had the situation been quite as grim as it became during the early 1990s. Cuba lacked currency from other countries, or foreign exchange, to pay for imports, including food and the oil and fertilizer needed for large-scale agriculture. The government strictly rationed food, but the meager amounts Cuban citizens received were barely enough to prevent widespread famine.

In the midst of this crisis, which the government dubbed the "Special Period," the Castro regime was forced to allow a dose of capitalism into Cuba's socialist economy. In order to acquire desperately needed foreign exchange, the government made a major push to promote tourism, and it concluded deals with foreign companies to develop hotels and resorts. The government also legalized the possession of U.S. dollars (which quickly became accepted for all purchases on the island) and allowed citizens to receive remittances (money sent from abroad). This created significant inequality: Cubans fortunate enough to have relatives in the United States who sent them money enjoyed a considerably higher standard of living than Cubans who didn't receive remittances.

During the Special Period, the Cuban government broke up huge state-run farms, turning them into smaller cooperatives. Farmers had to give a set amount of their harvest to the government, but anything they grew above and beyond their quota was theirs to eat—or even to sell. The government also made self-employment legal for certain categories of service work. If they obtained the necessary license, Cubans could, for example, repair appliances, operate a food stand, cut hair, or run a bed and breakfast for tourists out of their home.

By the late 1990s, the Cuban economy had emerged from the wreckage of the Special Period. The island got a further economic boost in 2000, when the socialist president of Venezuela, Hugo Chávez, agreed to a trade deal with Cuba. The terms were highly favorable to Cuba. In exchange for sending some 30,000 Cuban doctors, dentists, and nurses to Venezuela, Cuba would receive more than enough oil to meet its energy needs.

A TIME OF REFORMS

With the economy back on a sound footing, Fidel Castro sought to restore a purer form of socialism by reining in the limited free enterprise that had been introduced during the Special Period. In 2004, for instance, the issuance of new licenses was halted in dozens of self-employment categories. Cuba's budding

THE ECONOMY OF CUBA

Gross domestic product (GDP)[1]: $128.5 billion (2014 est.)
   agriculture (3.9% of GDP)—sugar, tobacco, citrus, coffee, rice, potatoes, beans; livestock
   industry (23% of GDP)—petroleum, nickel, cobalt, pharmaceuticals, tobacco, construction, steel, cement, agricultural machinery, sugar
   services (72.2% of GDP)

GDP per capita[1]: $11,600 (2014 est.)

Exports: $3.428 billion (petroleum, nickel, medical products, sugar, tobacco, fish, citrus, coffee)

Imports: $12.34 billion (petroleum, food, machinery and equipment, chemicals)

Inflation rate (consumer prices): 4.5%

Currency exchange rate: 1 Cuban peso (CUP) = 1 US dollar

[1] Purchasing power parity method. All figures are 2016 estimates unless otherwise indicated. Source: Adapted from CIA World Factbook, 2017.

entrepreneurs were put on notice by an official statement noting that certain private economic activities might again "be assimilated . . . by the state sector."

However, after Fidel Castro stepped down in 2008, it became apparent that his brother had different views regarding the Cuban economy. Raúl Castro was no less devoted to socialism. But, he said, socialism didn't require state control of all economic activity. Rather, it was sufficient for the state to "keep ownership of the fundamental means of production," like raw materials, factory facilities, and heavy machinery.

EDUCATIONAL VIDEO

Scan here for a look at market-based economic reforms introduced in Cuba:

Cuba's "absolutist" approach to socialism, in the new president's view, had created a bloated, inefficient state sector. Further, the Cuban people had come to expect the government to take care of them regardless of whether or not they were productive workers.

Raúl Castro sought to rid Cuba of unprofitable state enterprises, cut the number of Cubans employed by the state, boost the self-employment sector, and, as he remarked, "erase forever the notion that Cuba is the only country in the world where one can live without working." Castro spearheaded a series of reforms that, while relatively modest in scope and not always fully implemented, were intended to be irreversible.

In September 2010, for example, the Cuban government announced that half a million state-sector jobs would be slashed by May of 2011. Some of the laid-off workers would be reassigned to other state-sector positions. But most, it was hoped, would be absorbed into an expanding non-state sector. The government promised to relax regulations on self-employment and broaden opportunities in the private sector.

Cuba fell short of its 2011 layoff target, cutting only 140,000 state-sector jobs by year's end. However, the government's efforts to reduce state payrolls continued, and by 2015 more than 500,000 state-sector jobs had been eliminated.

Meanwhile, other reforms were slowly changing the face of

Cuba's economy. A 2011 measure established the beginnings of a private real-estate market. It permitted, for the first time since the revolution, the buying and selling of homes. A related measure directed Cuban banks to make home-repair loans. The government hoped that stimulating private investment would improve Cuba's housing stock—which is insufficient to accommodate the country's population and, in many areas, dilapidated—as well as boost self-employment in home repair. Another 2011 reform was designed to increase agricultural productivity. It allowed farmers to lease from the state up to 165 acres (67 hectares) of land, and to cultivate that land for their own profit. One way farmers took advantage was by growing fresh produce to sell to hotels.

In 2016, in what some observers believed was a pivotal step, the Cuban government announced that all entrepreneurs would be permitted to hire non–family members as employees. That practice had previously been legal only in certain lines of work. By officially sanctioning private hiring, the government hoped to expand the non-state sector from one characterized by self-employment to one in which small or even medium-sized private businesses might thrive.

ONGOING PROBLEMS

The reforms undertaken under Raúl Castro's leadership have yielded some noteworthy results. By 2016, for example, it was estimated that more than one-fourth of Cuba's workforce participated in the non-state sector.

Yet a brighter economic future for the island was by no means assured. Growth took a major hit in 2016, after an economic and political crisis in Venezuela compelled that country to dramatically cut its heavily *subsidized* oil exports to Cuba. Many economists took the Cuban government to task for failing to prepare for that eventuality. "It was clear the Venezuelan crisis at some point would have a negative impact on the Cuban economy," noted Pavel Vidal, a Cuban economist who teaches in Colombia. "Nevertheless, the commercial and financial dependence on Venezuela remained high and not enough was done to search for alternatives."

Workers roll cigars at a Cuban factory.

Beyond the unanticipated loss of Venezuelan oil, though, Cuba's economy is beset by chronic difficulties. The agricultural sector remains inefficient. Nearly one in five Cubans in the labor force works in agriculture. Yet agriculture accounts for only about 4 percent of gross domestic product. And despite fertile soil, Cuba imports about 80 percent of its food.

Tourism is now the mainstay of Cuba's economy. More than 3.5 million foreigners visited the island in 2015, and the numbers were projected to grow in succeeding years because of the U.S. government's easing of travel restrictions to Cuba for American citizens. But the money brought by tourists has led to some unforeseen consequences. A Cuban state-sector worker makes, on average, the equivalent of only about $20 to $25 per month. Yet Cubans who cater to tourists and have access to tips can easily make many times that amount. This has produced a sort of small-scale "brain drain," with highly trained professionals quitting their state-sector jobs for tourist-related self-employment. In Cuba, it's not at all uncommon for a doctor to drive a cab, or an engineer to wait tables.

Meanwhile, material circumstances for the majority of Cubans continue to be difficult. Many get by only through the monthly *libreta de racionamiento*, or ration book, which the government has been giving all citizens for decades and which entitles them to modest amounts of staples such as rice, cooking oil, and beans at subsidized prices.

TEXT-DEPENDENT QUESTIONS

1. Identify some problems Cuba encountered in its efforts to implement a socialist economy.
2. What caused the economic crisis known as the "Special Period"?
3. Why did the 2016 economic and political crisis in Venezuela hurt Cuba's economy?

RESEARCH PROJECT

Cuba's economy is now highly dependent on tourism. Using the Internet, see if you can find the number of annual visitors to the island over several years. Present the results in graph form.

The modern skyline of Havana, as seen from the Spanish colonial-era fort known as El Morro that guards the harbor. Havana is Cuba's capital and main commercial center. It is also the island's largest city, home to nearly 20 percent of Cuba's population.

📖 WORDS TO UNDERSTAND IN THIS CHAPTER

census—an official count of a country's population.

genetic—relating to genes, the sequences of DNA that control inherited traits.

travelogue—a narrated motion picture about travel, or a book about travel.

PEOPLE AND COMMUNITIES

The Cuban people have a reputation for taking great joy in life. A deep love of music and dance permeates Cuban culture. And many visitors to the island have been struck by Cubans' easy sociability.

The makeup of Cuba's population reflects the legacies of Spanish colonization and slavery on the island. In 2012, according to the country's *census*, 64.1 percent of the Cuban population was white, 9.3 percent was black, and 26.6 percent was of mixed ancestry (any combination of white, black, and indigenous). But the Cuban census counts race based on citizens' self-identification. *Genetic* studies suggest that few Cubans are exclusively white or black. Rather, the vast majority have European, African, and indigenous ancestors.

As of 2016, Cuba's population was estimated at about 11.2 million. That represented a decline of more than 300,000 from the previous year's figure. Large numbers of Cubans had been leaving the island since the government's 2013 decision to eliminate the requirement that citizens obtain an exit visa in order to travel abroad. Many hoped to settle in the United States. However, that became more difficult after January 2017, when President Barack Obama ended the U.S. policy by which virtually any Cuban who reached U.S. soil—even without a valid visa—would automatically be eligible for permanent-residency status.

HAVANA

Cuba's capital city, Havana (Spanish: La Habana), is home to more than 2.1 million souls—or nearly one of every five Cubans. Havana is Cuba's commercial center, the island's main port, and a province unto itself.

The conquistador Diego Velásquez founded a settlement called San Cristóbal de la Habana on the southwestern coast of Cuba in 1515. But the settlement failed to thrive, and in 1519 San Cristóbal de la Habana was moved to its current location along a bay in northwestern Cuba. The advantages as a port were obvious: the bay consisted of a narrow inlet that opened into a broad natural harbor. Havana, established on the western end of the bay, was plundered by French pirates in the 1520s and 1530s, and burned to the ground in 1555.

After that, Spain constructed a series of fortifications to protect Havana. The city, which became capital of the Cuba colony in 1607, served as the hub for Spain's "treasure

THE PEOPLE OF CUBA

Population: 11,179,995 (July 2016 est.)

Ethnic groups: white 64.1%, mestizo 26.6%, black 9.3% (2012 est.)

Population growth rate: -0.3%

Birth rate: 10.8 births/1,000 population

Death rate: 8.6 deaths/1,000 population

Age structure:
  0–14 years: 16.7%
  15–24 years: 12.44%
  25–54 years: 44.95%
  55–64 years: 11.27%
  65 years and over: 14.64%
  Median age: 41.1 years

Life expectancy at birth:
  total population: 78.7 years
  male: 76.4 years
  female: 81.1 years

Literacy: 99.8% (age 15 and over can read and write)

All figures are 2016 estimates unless otherwise indicated.
Source: CIA World Factbook, 2017.

fleets"—annual convoys of ships transporting gold, silver, and other coveted goods from the New World colonies to Spain. As such, Havana was one of the most important cities in the Spanish Empire, and it grew wealthy. It also expanded, mostly to the south and west, over the course of centuries.

Cubans walk through a dilapidated neighborhood in Havana. Many Cubans live in poverty, although government subsidies of food and essential items mean that they are better off than the extremely poor in other countries.

A period of rapid growth occurred during the early decades of the 20th century, after Cuba gained independence. Havana was a popular tourist destination, known for its elegance as well as its exciting nightlife, up until the Cuban Revolution.

Under communist rule, large portions of Havana fell into disrepair. Once-luxurious hotels and nightclubs became dilapidated. Centuries-old colonial buildings crumbled.

The reopening of Cuba to large-scale tourism has led to a boom in new-hotel construction in Havana. Additionally, the Cuban government has been working to restore and redevelop Habana Vieja (Old Havana), a UNESCO World Heritage Site. With its narrow cobblestone streets, 16th-century forts, and colonial architecture, Old Havana is a natural draw for visitors. The Vedado district, built largely during the 20th century, is also a popular tourist area. It features restaurants, nightclubs, and shops.

Havana's residential neighborhoods range from upscale to impoverished. For example, the Playa district—located in the northwestern part of the city, along the coast—is a conspicuously well-to-do area. It's home to many foreign diplomats and business owners. By contrast, Centro Habana (Central Havana)—located between Old Havana and Vedado—is crowded and decaying.

EDUCATIONAL VIDEO

This *travelogue*, filmed in the 1930s, explores Havana:

OTHER MAJOR CITIES

Santiago de Cuba, capital of the province of the same name, is the island's second-largest city and an important seaport. At year's end 2014, according to Cuba's Oficina Nacional de Estadística e Información (Office of National Statistics and Information), Santiago de Cuba had an urban population of 456,786. (Cuban municipalities also include surrounding rural areas, but the figures presented here are for the cities proper.)

Located along the southeastern coast, Santiago de Cuba was founded in 1515 by Diego Velázquez. It served as colonial Cuba's first capital.

Thousands of tourists visit the Holy Trinity Church in Trinidad every year.

Pedestrians walk through the main square of Santiago de Cuba.

Fleeing the Haitian Revolution, a large number of French planters—along with enslaved Africans and free blacks—settled in Santiago de Cuba during the 1790s. That influence can still be felt in the city's unique culture. The city was the birthplace of some of Cuba's most important music and dance styles, and its annual carnival celebration (held in July) is renowned. Santiago de Cuba's San Pedro de la Roca Castle, completed in 1638, is a UNESCO World Heritage Site.

Camagüey (2014 population: 307,143) is the capital of central Cuba's Camagüey Province. Camagüey was established at its current location—on a plain far inland—in 1528, after an

View of Camagüey's Sacred Heart of Jesus Cathedral. Cuba's third-largest city was designated a UNESCO World Heritage Centre in 2008.

earlier settlement on the northern coast had to be abandoned because of repeated pirate attacks. Camagüey is known for its winding streets, pleasant squares, and multitude of churches. The city's center has been designated a UNESCO World Heritage Site.

With a 2014 population of just under 300,000, Holguín ranks as Cuba's fourth-largest city. It, too, is a provincial capital; Holguín Province is situated in northeastern Cuba. To the north of the city are a number of beach resorts.

Cuba had two other cities with more than 200,000 residents in 2014. Guantánamo (220,146) is the capital of Cuba's easternmost province, also named Guantánamo. Santa Clara (222,027) is the capital of central Cuba's Villa Clara Province.

TEXT-DEPENDENT QUESTIONS

1. What part of Havana has been designated a World Heritage Site by UNESCO?
2. Name Cuba's second-largest city. Where on the island is it located?
3. Why was the settlement of Camagüey moved inland in 1528?

RESEARCH PROJECT

Read about one of Cuba's 15 provinces. Write a short travelogue about its capital city.

Series Glossary

asylee—in the United States, an alien who receives asylum, meeting the legal definition of an individual who is unable or unwilling to return to his or her home country due to a fear of persecution on account of race, religion, nationality, political opinion, or membership in a particular social group.

asylum—protection granted by a government to a refugee from another country.

authoritarian—favoring blind submission to authority.

capitalism—an economic system that permits the ownership of private property, allows individuals and companies to compete for their own economic gain, and generally lets free market forces determine the price of goods and services.

communism—a political and economic system that champions the elimination of private property and common ownership of goods, for the benefit of all members of society.

deportation—the formal removal of an alien after he or she has broken immigration laws.

ideology—a systematic set of principles and goals.

indoctrination—instruction in the basic principles of a political party or other organization.

lobby—an organized attempt to convince a legislator to vote a certain way on an issue.

nationalism—a sense of national consciousness; promotion of the interests of one's own nation above the interests of other nations.

paramilitary—relating to a force organized along military lines but not composed of official soldiers.

proletariat—the class of industrial workers.

refugee—a person who is unable or unwilling to return to his or her country of nationality because of persecution or a well-founded fear of persecution.

socialism—an economic system that is based on cooperation rather than competition and that utilizes centralized planning and distribution, controlled by the government; in Marxist theory, an intermediate stage between capitalism and communism during which the state—controlled by the proletariat—owns all factories and other places of work, and wages and the distribution of goods are still somewhat unequal.

totalitarian—relating to a political regime that seeks to exert complete control over citizens' lives.

Further Reading

Cooke, Julia. *The Other Side of Paradise: Life in the New Cuba*. Berkeley, CA: Seal Press, 2014.

Mesa-Lago, Carmelo, and Jorge Pérez-López. *Cuba Under Raúl Castro: Assessing the Reforms*. Boulder, CO: Lynne Rienner Publishers, 2013.

Pérez, Louis A., Jr. *Cuba: Between Reform and Revolution*. 5th ed. New York: Oxford University Press, 2015.

Sánchez, Yoani, and M. J. Porter (translator). *Havana Real: One Woman Fights to Tell the Truth About Cuba Today*. Brooklyn, NY: Melville House Publishing, 2011.

Sweig, Julia E. *Cuba: What Everyone Needs to Know*. New York: Oxford University Press, 2009.

Valladares, Armando. *Against All Hope: A Memoir of Life in Castro's Gulag*. New York: Encounter Books, 2001.

Internet Resources

www.brookings.edu/topic/cuba/
Reports on various aspects of Cuba today—including the economy, social conditions, and relations with the United States—from the Brookings Institution, a think tank based in Washington, D.C.

http://oncubamagazine.com/en/#
The Internet version of *OnCuba*, a monthly magazine published in Miami. *OnCuba*, which maintains a news bureau in Havana, features stories about economic matters, society, culture, and more.

http://en.granma.cu/cuba
The English version of *Granma*, the official newspaper of Cuba's ruling Communist Party.

www.cia.gov/library/publications/the-world-factbook/geos/cu.html
The CIA World Factbook's Cuba page contains basic information about the island's geography, government, people and society, economy, and more.

Index

Numbers in ***bold italic*** refer to captions.

About the Author: John Ziff, a freelance writer and editor, has long been interested in Latin American history and culture. He lives outside Philadelphia.

Picture Credits: Everett Collection: 22, 27, 38; Library of Congress: 35, 36; used under license from Shutterstock, Inc.: 2, 6, 9, 10, 13, 14, 18, 25, 29, 31, 32, 42, 52, 64, 70, 72; Giuseppe Crimeni / Shutterstock.com: 23; Diego Grandi / Shutterstock.com: 45; Frederic Legrand — COMEO / Shutterstock.com: 46; Felix Lipov / Shutterstock.com: 3, 56; Lulu and Isabelle / Shutterstock.com: 1; Lunasee Studios / Shutterstock.com: 62; Julian Peters Photography / Shutterstock.com: 71; Matyas Rehak / Shutterstock.com: 68; Riderfoot / Shutterstock.com: 49; Jakub Travel Photo / Shutterstock.com: 55; United Nations photo: 20; U.S. Coast Guard photo: 40; official White House photo: 39.